The State of Black Women:

All for One

or

All for Self?

Cathy L. Webb

Dedication

To every Black female soul that shines bright when alone but her brightest when amongst kindred spirits...

* With each breath, we must believe in the goodness, strength, and beauty of the Black Queen. Without it, we shall have no progress. *

Purpose of this book

This book is written to Black Queens everywhere. It is my hope that the words will spark conversations and actions on self-love, womanhood, sisterhood, and the need for personal accountability.

Chapter one looks at how we are defined by others and ourselves, how our perspective and mindset shifted, and the importance of unity with our Black Men.

Chapter two analyzes how we use our voice and appearance to present ourselves, and the impact of Black Women collaborations and relationships.

The Black Queen's inner beings are the focus of chapter three. It focuses on how our decisions and actions are influenced by them.

External aspects of the world and how they influence and impact our lives for the short- and long-term are discussed in chapter four.

Each chapter concludes with "Questions to Ponder" which can be used as part of a personal self-discovery journey or for a group discussion. These ae aspects of our being and lives need open and honest discussions...today!

To future conversations with yourselves and each other,

Cathy L. Webb

A Proud Black African Queen

Table of Content

Dedication................................3

Purpose of This Book.....................5

Chapter I: The Black Woman 11
a. Self-awareness

b. Society's description

c. Generational transitions

d. Black Unity

Chapter II: Black Women............21
a. Presentation

b. Conversation

c. Collaboration

d. Relationships

Chapter III: Internal Shackles.......31

a. Self-love

b. Self-worth

c. Self-confidence

d. Self-defeating Habits

Chapter IV: External Bondage......41

a. Family/Friends

b. Relationships

c. Career

d. Church/Religion

Personal Declaration.....................51

Answering the Question.................53

References......................55

About the Author...............57

Books..................59

Contact..................60

Love the person you see every morning!

Chapter I: The Black Woman

Who is the Black Woman? What makes her unique? Why is she worth being talked about, given the spotlight, and applauded? Society tries to respond to these questions using terms, phrases, or images with negative connotations. It depicts the Black Woman as angry or aggressive; says she is too independent, so men steer clear of her presence. According to "everyone else," the Black Woman is the epitome of sadness and degradation, deserves nothing from life but pity, and should be mocked for everything she has, does, wears, thinks, and says, especially if it goes against the status quo. There is little to no value of or appreciation for her.

With all this on her shoulders and her mind, how does the Black Woman survive in this world? How does she step out with her beautiful mahogany skin glistening and wear a Colgate smile while doing so? How does she show up and show out every day? It's quite simple actually! She knows that no one can give her an identity. She defines who she is and creates her own narrative. She determines how she will live life without self-imposed limits. The Black Queen knows how to express her creativity and individuality while living her vision. There is no status quo living in her space!

The Black Woman has a high level of self-awareness. She knows her roots are based in a long line of strong Black Women. When she experiences a moment of weakness, she draws from their strength. She recalls what her ancestors endured so she could experience true freedom. Nothing she faces compares to what they endured. They survived years of emotional, physical, and psychological abuse so she could handle a challenging work situation or a difficult person. With a smile, she silently thanks them for their sacrifices, exhales, and keeps moving forward.

Every Black Woman describes herself in a positive way. Why would she not? She knows how amazing she is and how her life affects others. Her self-made Queen's blueprint that she follows to reach her destiny. She owns and stands in "hers," whatever that looks like. None the less, she is not an island and must interact with those outside of herself. We must then ask, "How does the world perceive the Black Woman?"

For many, it is mostly a negative thought or feeling. Expressing strong emotions is labeled as loud, angry, aggressive, stubborn, and argumentative. These stereotypical terms are viewed in a more attractive way when displayed by other races (for example "loud" becomes "outspoken" and "stubborn" becomes "strong-willed"). In full disclosure, I have used these words to describe other Black Women. For this, I am ashamed (bald head bowed). Today, I stop myself from doing what many others do. Instead of using a single moment to bash a fellow Queen, we must make a conscious decision to applaud her.

Set in your mind that she is strength, power, brilliance, beauty, kindness, and royalty personified. She has persevered through life and her light remains bright. When you see a Black

Queen who appears to be struggling, acknowledge her with a smile, "hello," or a complement. This could make a huge difference in her day. The Black Queen is the foundation of this world and bears the fruit of life. Celebrate one another simply because we exist.

No Black Woman is exempt from criticism. Remember how the media used harsh words to describe our Forever First Lady Michelle Obama? Her spouse held the highest political office in the country for eight years yet daggers of hatred were thrown at her. Their attempts to make her feel less than all failed. How did she respond? With nothing but respect, grace, and positivity!! She knew who she was and never allowed others to write her narrative. With each word and action, Mrs. Obama revealed her strength and dignity. Today, she remains one of the most respected women in the world! How about that, Black Queen!

Speaking of celebrating one another, the Black Woman must ensure future generations of females feel and express a high level of self-awareness. This involves sharing our experiences but also listening as they speak about theirs. We must support and encourage them in their life's pursuits and help them avoid sacrificing who they were created to become. They have strong, powerful voices and should shout clearly and boldly, not whisper. When we value our voices and what we have to say, we can use it in positive ways to strengthen the bonds of sisterhood.

On the downside, our mindset has changed over the last couple of generations. For example, women are less concerned about how they present themselves. Years ago, women wore slips underneath dresses and skirts to flatten the panty line. Today, some accomplish this by not wearing underwear. Also, some women expose more skin with their clothing when they used to cover up. When leaving home, taking the time to present yourself in a nice way is less of a concern or desire today. Perhaps these external changes (and others) result from low self-respect or self-love.

Other factors that influenced the mindset of Women are the emergence of social media, easier access to education and other resources, and the lack of Black female community leaders. Social media showcases the "highs" of others' lives, and we see this a perceived lack on our part. Access to education and resources that allow us to increase our independence and close the gender gap makes the "family unit" obsolete to many. The lack of Black females in positions of power diminishes hope that our lives can change. Instead, it pushes us towards a greater sense of independence and the need to develop a "me and mine" mentality.

Another area where there has been a shift is the level of personal responsibility. Years ago, the Black Man worked to provide for his family (sometimes at the expense of not seeing them often). The Black Woman stayed home, raised the children, and cared for the home. She was satisfied spending her days at home doing for others. Today, many Black Women are forced to be independent and responsible for everything. Because she does, she does not feel a need to seek help. In fact, she may be offended if it is offered or suggested.

Today's Black Woman wants to be fulfilled and pursue her desires. Simply put, we want more and deserve it! Sometimes to get that "more" from life, uniting with other Black Women is necessary. When we unite and work for the betterment of ourselves and the world, look out! Something amazing is in the works. If society wants to stop this or write us off, they inject fear, doubt, and self-hatred into the mix in some manner. Inner work and outward strength are needed to combat this. Young ladies listen to your elders when they share wisdom. The mindset must change to point your life in a new direction. You are Queens so represent!

Although society continues to change, one facet of life we hope remains strong, steady, and constant is our bond with the Black Man. His love, respect, trust, and support are critical to our survival as Black people. How he views us often affects how we view ourselves. We subconsciously judge and are judged. This is a tough pill to swallow, but we must reveal our truth as it is lived and felt.

Although we should feel whole alone, his energy helps us feel complete. When he looks at us, what is he thinking? Does he still desire to become one with us? Raise a family with us? Decades ago, the response would have been a definite yes with no hesitation. The family was husband, wife, and many children. Through everything, they stood together. The husband took great pride in providing for his family. He was the head of the household in all aspects, and it was understood as such. There was no greater joy for the Black Man than to have a strong Black Woman by his side.

As time passes, this dynamic changes to suit current personal or societal norms. The connection between Black Men and Black Women, or just men and women in general, continues to diminish. It goes from mutual love and respect to tolerance and disregard.

Unfortunately, this is not reserved for any specific generation. Black Men and Black Women see one another as competition or obstacles to be eliminated. There is no desire to rebuild that which began to crumble long ago. There is no "We" or "Us," only "Me" and "Mine" when it comes to the Black Man and the Black Woman.

How do we rebuild our empire to create a legacy?

Questions to Ponder

a. What is your perception of the Black Woman?

b. Why do you believe society describes the Black Woman negatively?

c. Has there been a shift in the Black Woman's mindset? If so, what do you believe is responsible?

Chapter II: Black Women

According to Statista Research Department (2021), there was nearly 169 million women in the United States in 2019. Of this number, only 12.9% were classified as Black (Catalyst, 2021). Although all Black Women fit into one category, not all should receive the same label. This applies to every aspect of life and often carries a negative connotation affecting how they are perceived by others. Daily actions can be affected, including how they present themselves with their appearance, how they interact with one another, and their persona in relationships, personal and professional.

You see, I was told to make sure every strand of hair (yes, I had hair as a child and as an adult) and every piece of clothing are in place before leaving home. Not because you want to impress the world but because you respect yourself. Having three sisters, we all made sure we looked presentable. Our mom always said we were representing *her*, so we better make *her* look good. Funny thing is I say this to my 22-year-old daughter. This shows generational support, love, and wisdom. Keep it going Queens!

When I'm out, I observe other Black Women to gauge their personal and unique styles. One area that doesn't surprise me is the level of skin exposure in clothing. Items today are designed as short-lived trends, not long-term wear. What does shock me is the number of older Black Women wearing revealing, tight clothing. Perhaps this is how they showcase their body or an attempt to appear younger. This may also be seen as attractive to men. Regardless, the level of self-respect and self-worth continue to decrease and must be maximized. The female body is a temple and must be worshipped and protected, even from ourselves at times.

Looking deep, we understand that our life's circumstances are different. Black Women may be dealing with issues affecting their physical and mental spaces at any given time. Being physically exhausted is real. Mental strain is real. These impact her health and present themselves on her body and in her life. Without proper support in a timely manner, both can affect how she feels about herself over time. Make sure we check in on one another.

Other ways Black Women present themselves is with the color and style of their hair. Their crown has no tongue, but it speaks volumes. It showcases her mood and expresses her pride and confidence. These Queens have an amazing ability to create masterpieces with every strand. We do not always appreciate the versatility of the crown, but we are no longer changing it to suit the preferences of others. They try to imitate it but there is nothing like the Black Queen's crown.

Not only does the style of her crown speak volumes, so does her tongue. As children, we were taught to be silent in the company of others and in public. Today, we know that the collective power of Black Women's voices gets stronger with time. This means more to the world when the conversation is relevant and about a topic that positively affects others. What we speak about is what our soul contains. The inside of the heart is revealed when the mouth opens. We must use our power to speak life and energy into the world.

On the other side, being loud for the sake of being seen is never good. It causes others to think less of you. Unfortunately, some Black Women do not understand or care how their behaviors impact all Black Women. Perhaps they do not believe anything is wrong. This way of thinking or lack of concern must be addressed. We must work to better understand how-to walk-through life as a Queen while still being authentic. If we are to continue evolving and progressing as a group, we must use our powerful voices to empower and inspire those around us. Let them know they do not have to shrink and appear calmer or be "more ladylike" to be heard.

Speaking of empowering others, the nurturing souls of Black Women causes them to help other women progress. Collaboration that is positive and mutually beneficial is an essential key to strengthening the bonds of sisterhood. Expanding this to include the younger generation of Black females matters as they are affected by our decisions. They are more prone to being impacted by our everchanging environment. This means the OG Black Women are needed now more than ever.

Self-serving Black Women see other Black Women's actions and moves as competition. Instead of being happy for and supportive of their success, they seek ways to counteract or destroy their reputation. Often with the help of other Black Women. They decide that one less competitor increases their chance for success. This could not be further from the truth. Instead, be confident in the person you are and all you have achieved. Then you can stand to clap for others without pretending.

The level of collaboration depends upon how each Black Woman perceives the others. If they are determined to support and elevate each other and are committed to building it, the work will be positive and long-lasting. Building her own table (legacy) is the goal of every Black Woman owned business. Doing so with a group of like-minded Black Queens is even sweeter. This can begin with the simple act of speaking to one another. You never know the Black Girl magic a simple "hello" could create. We can dream it, plan it, and launch it.

Then again, there are some Black Women who prefer to work solo or with those who do not look like her. Perhaps she was in a past situation that did not end well, or she was taken advantage of. Maybe there is a lack of trust or wanting to ask for help. These reasons and many others can impact her desire to work with other Black Women, especially those she does not already know.

Collaborating with friends means mutual trust and respect already exist. Having a long-standing friendship is rare today. Maybe the ladies are unaware of how to uplift one another, or they stick with the ideology of "competition over collaboration." When you're young, you give everyone the title "friend." As you age, you realize having "true" friends is more important than having "lots of" friends. Making friends when you're older can be less authentic. Another issue is some women are quicker to forgive a man before another woman. Without it, a small issue can ruin a friendship. Having friendships from your younger years means they know and accepted the real you. Isn't this what friendship is all about?

One aspect of the Black Woman that many perceive as negative is her independence. Many operate as single, not by choice but by force. Allow me to explain. Her companion is no longer with her, so she is forced to handle the challenges of motherhood alone. After a few less-than-ideal relationships, she may choose to stay single. Expressing this instantly draws criticism and negativity. She's told she is too picky or tries to "do too much." Queen, never settle for the sake of "having a man." There's too much at stake to accept anything less than who you deserve and who deserves to enter your space. Pew Research Center (2021) states that 32% of Black homes had a Black Woman at the head in 2019. By choice or by force? You decide.

We are a powerful force! The world knows this and tries to stop or slow down our progress at every turn. It knows and understands our strength and power and seeks to use it against us. Attempts to instill fear and cause us to see ourselves as negative all fail. When we lack knowledge of our potential or do not trust ourselves, we accept life's crumbs instead of moving mountains. If we allow their words into our mental space, we will begin to believe what they say. We must keep this truth in the front of our minds. Yeah, we say it but do we truly believe it? Do we act on it once we do? A few, but many Black Women go through the motions of living and loving themselves. This must end...NOW!

Come with me my sister so we can chat right quick! Hear me and hear me good...ANYTHING THAT NEGATIVELY AFFECTS YOUR FAITH, FAMILY, FINANCES, OR PHYSICAL AND MENTAL HEALTH IS NOT WORTH YOUR TIME! Be selfish when it comes to these aspects.

Know what to allow into your space and what to keep on the other side of the boundary you created. The beautiful and confident Black Woman in the mirror IS you. Period.

Questions to Ponder

a. Why are some Black Women not presenting themselves in a positive way?

b. Why do you believe more Black Women don't focus on finding and using their voice?

c. Why do you believe some Black female friendships end?

Chapter III: Internal Shackles

Looking at a Black Woman, you may see her as who the world told you she is or based on your own interactions with others. Her emotions may determine how she "puts herself together" each day. You see her physically but lack knowledge of her soul or what she desires from life and others. Her soul is invisible to the naked eye and only presents itself through actions. On one hand, the Black Woman does an excellent job of using material accessories to highlight her external beauty. On the other, what she carries inside is of greater importance and calls for self-reflections throughout life. These invisible shackles determine if she accepts her purpose or wallows in self-pity in a comfort zone.

How you care for your personal space often defines the level of care you have for yourself as a Woman. This is characterized as self-love. Placing yourself at the top of your list of things and/or people to care for is seen as being selfish. Some believe other people are more important and deserve to come first. What many fail to realize is, it is impossible to give to others when your energy and spirit are depleted. You cannot give that which is not within you. Sharing any part of yourself demands wholeness and balance from the soul.

How can you feel whole when your self-perception is negative? In the mirror, your eyes go straight to what you perceive as flaws. Years of being programmed or brainwashed is the culprit. Social media makes you think people worldwide have "made it" while you continue to "get by" or that you need to do and be better. Start to live as who you are or see the good inside you. Your already low self-love spirals downward. I urge you to not personalize others' success as a knock against your life. Instead, continue working on you from the soul. Everything will fall into place. You got this Sis!

So how can you as a Black Woman make sure your soul is healthy, balanced, and positive? How do you ensure your fellow Queens are also filled with nothing but royal items? Answering these questions demands looking at yourself as a dual threat...an inner goddess with a royal soul and an outer beauty with a melanin glow! You must identify your soul's additives (what it needs to be improved) and preservatives (what it needs to be maintained). When you know these, spoil your soul with love and attention. "Soul revivals" are welcomed and encouraged. Queen, you are the complete package!

First, accept yourself mentally and emotionally as one who can accomplish what is before you. The actions you take start within your mind. Your inner conversation dictates how you spend your time. Straighten out your thinking. You can step into the world and make life happen or you can stay home and complain about what you lack. The choice is yours. This decision is a precursor to an increased self-awareness and self-confidence. With these, you can identify relevant strategies and actions to design the life you deserve. It starts by not letting the world tamper with your feelings and thinking.

This starts in childhood with the environment you grow up in. We are extremely impressionable as children. Everything we see and hear impacts us later as it defines what we classify as "normal," whether positive or negative. When your self-esteem and self-worth are low, you may allow behaviors to influence your decisions; behaviors that prevent a positive self-perspective.

When you know your value, you know it is not defined by material possessions. They do not increase your status in life, provide a true sense of accomplishment, or make you more successful or valuable as a person. The truth is you may feel empty inside and are trying to fill the void externally. Instead of trying to look put together on the outside for the world, get your soul, heart, and mind together for you. Let that radiate outward. Then you'll have a new balanced and authentic you.

Your new life is not going to pop up overnight. It will take plenty of time, hard work, and determination. Second thing to remember is consistent, repetitive actions will be required. There are no shortcuts to success (however you define it). Some Black Women strive for a life lived by society's definition of success (abundance of material possessions). Others know what has real value and what has a price tag. Many believe a successful life will cause others to view them differently. Since we seek others' approval, we stay in our comfort zone where life is familiar, and change is rare.

As time progresses and life becomes more challenging, many Black people, especially Women, work harder to change the direction of their lives. They seek more education, increase their skill sets, move into executive-level positions, and start businesses. An increasing self-love and a determination to care for themselves and their families long-term are motivating factors in the Black Queen community.

On the other side, many Black Women are content in their current position or role, so they settle for the minimum. This goes for relationships, careers, and education, to name a few.

They settle into the traditional gender roles that society still believe in and push for (women at home with the children, men work to provide). If the woman works, she faces the wage gap. To avoid this, the world suggests women focus on their appearance to "land a man" to get taken care of. Advancing herself is on the bottom of her priorities list for some Black Women, if it's on it at all! Queen, this is the old way of thinking! Do you Sis! You can do it!

Another rarity is a confident Black Woman who does not cater to the whims of this world. She accepts that there is no badge of shame to being draped in beautiful Black skin. This Black Woman can merge into the world without losing who she is. Yes, there are some who fit this bill, but there could be more. Many Black Women choose belonging and fitting in over standing out and standing on their own. This is because they fear ridicule if they separate from the group. In this case, freedom to be yourself is just a phrase as they lack courage to do what's necessary to live it.

Being able to stand alone comes with an increased level of self-confidence. When you know who you are and what you can accomplish, you will allow nothing and no one to stand between you and your goals. This confidence may diminish as the process proceeds but when you see the light at the end, your determination intensifies. Your confidence reaches an all-new level when the goal is achieved. It helps you set new goals and begin again.

Self-defeating habits often hinder progress. These are actions (or inactions) we take (or not take) that impact the success level of our goals. Many times, we do not realize we are engaging in these actions. Something happens that forces us to see what we've been doing (or not doing). Then we can analyze the actions' impact and influence on our lives and take corrective actions immediately to mitigate long-term damage.

No matter what Black Queen, never forget that you are a global phenomenon! You can shake up this planet without opening your mouth. Your presence says it all! Be sure to snag moments of happiness when they happen to enjoy the spontaneous joy of being alive. Let that sink in as you prepare yourself for the challenges of. life. No matter. You are ready! You got this!

Questions to Ponder

a. Why do many Black Women have a negative self-perception?

b. How does a Black Woman's childhood affect her self-perception?

c. Are Black Women less likely to seek ways to improve their lives?

"Love the person you see every morning!"

Chapter IV: External Bondage

After examining and refining her soul, the Black Women turns her attention to what is outside her that affects and influences her. What we engage in and who we interact with plays a role in our decision-making. Some of these influences we have a little control over while others are completely in the hands of someone else. How to handle them? Realize your reaction is what matters and you can minimize their impact on your life. This ensures each day is lived according to your standards.

Our primary external influencer is family. You have those you were born related to (parents, siblings, extended relatives) and those you choose to be related to (spouse, in-laws, children). Their words and actions either support or disrupt your decisions and actions. Sure, family members disagree but there must be mutual respect. When this is missing or is replaced with disregard, separation can result in the hopes of gaining peace. If reconciliation is not possible, continued distance may be the solution. Do what work for your life Queen!

No matter what, your upbringing will impact your life's decisions. You feed off your environment and the people you spent time with. This will define your idea of "normal." Living in a loving home or one filled with negativity increases the chances of you living the same way. You can place yourself in negative situations later in life or you can do the opposite to avoid the same results. This way the cycle is broken.

We all have toxic, fearful, and untrusting people in our family who are clueless about who they are. Be mindful of their influence. Often, we settle for less than what we desire to make others happy or show respect for their opinions or something they've done for us. In these moments, we lose a sense of self. Since you can't choose your family, ensure any negativity does not impact your soul. Establish balance and live as you choose by creating healthy boundaries, staying true to self, and maintaining a bond of love and respect.

When you have a female friend who you call sister, she is the first person you call when you need to "exhale." Her unwavering support and encouragement mean the world to you and your heart! The two of you are two halves of one whole. If you have more than one, you are truly special! What is said, positive or negative, to you or about your life matters. It can cause you to work harder or stop dead in your tracks. You may get upset but later realize it was what you needed in that moment. Thanks girl!

Speaking of an influencer of your choosing, your romantic partner can build you up with love, support, and encouragement to grow and better yourself. This is what every Black Woman hope to have when she begins a relationship. It will not take long for you to understand the type of person they are. Their values in life will become evident. Never stay in denial or let someone tamper with your present or future. It means too much to the world.

They can also tear you down by spewing words to destroy your self-confidence and self-worth. Anything that feels toxic is toxic. Time to step up or step back. If you choose to remain in this toxic situation, you lose a part of who you are today and hinder who you were created to become tomorrow. Perhaps, you are unable to get out or believes it is all you deserve. What's worse is if you do not view the relationship as toxic because it imitates your childhood norm. Many women are pushed to start a family, so they settle for this. They may settle for involvement with someone else's partner and tell themselves "A piece of a man is better than no man." No Queen it is not. You deserve better! You're worth more!

Staying in a relationship not conducive to your personal growth disrupts your upward mobility and keeps you stuck in a comfort zone. There is no aspiration for more than what is in front of you. If there is, no actions are taken, only talked about. You complain but make no changes to your habits or lifestyle. Your words fall on closed ears as no one pays attention when you talk about the future.

For some Black Women, that future involves a new career or a promotion within the current one. Their sights are set on sitting at *that* table. They do everything possible to prove themselves and impress the boss. Unfortunately, they remain overlooked or receive an arbitrary reason why now is "not their time." Instead of reacting, they placate the office to avoid receiving the "angry Black Woman" label. In addition, some level of racism and sexism appears if there are white men at the top. Years pass and they are stuck or lose the desire to advance professionally. Their confidence has been decreased and their emotional and mental health are affected. They failed to recognize who they are as a Black Woman. Get up and go!

In 2020, Black Women were at the top of only 4.1% of all management positions in the U.S. (Catalyst, 2021). This means the time has come to get a large, mahogany table and queen style seats for the executive suite of your own business. Stop depending on others to dictate your career path. Carve out your own and make it wide enough for your sisters to join you if they choose.

When any part of life feels out of balance, the Black Woman often turns to her spiritual foundation for guidance and support. She knows that her soul is the foundation of who she is and what she stands for. It gives her strength to get through each day. Sometimes we fall short of being the Woman we want to be, but we can acknowledge that and pledge to do and be better going forward.

Where does this deep-rooted faith come from? Generations before taught us through their words and actions to always turn to the Creator. Throughout our lives, our mothers, grandmothers, aunties, and "big mamas" showed us how to survive and make whatever we need out of very little. Many still follow this but others follow a more spiritual path. Having a foundation to rely on is what keeps many Black Women's heads above water and allows them to breathe.

Some say faith and religion can be a problem for many Black Women. It can push them to settle in relationships and procreate because the Bible says that is what they are here to do. It should state for the partner to be your husband, a man of the church, and the relationship to be loving, mutually respectful, and supportive. Without these, priorities change, and life becomes more complicated.

Somewhere along the way, the desire to attend church services, congregate with believers, or study the Bible faded. Many blame the church's constant push for members to give more and more financially or the pastor's messages on less spiritual-based issues (ex. politics). This leads to reduced attendance. Not saying that one should follow a specific religious/spiritual path; simply have a "being" that you connect with to stay grounded. Otherwise, life may swallow you and leave your bones on the curb!

Who and what you are connected to affects how you move through life. If those around you are satisfied "just getting by," their behaviors will eventually affect you. Your career may provide financial support, but your spiritual foundation is unstable. When these aspects of life are disconnected you experience a "soul imbalance." Any desire or action to reconnect your life may be shot down, mocked, or simply not work. You're left feeling like the only option is to settle. Many Black Women do just that. Time to get out of that mindset Queens!

Know your value as a Black Woman. External changes and validations only offer instant gratification. This is fine for some but not for Black Queens. We deserve much more and will make sure we get it. Remind each other that all you can control in life is how you respond to life...emotionally, physically, and mentally. There are options but the final decision rests with you. Choose wisely Queen! When you accept your past and define your present, you are laying claim to creating your future.

Questions to Ponder

a. Why do some Black Women settle for toxic relationships?

b. How and why are Black Women negatively influenced by family/friends?

c. Can faith influence the Black Woman to settle desires? If so, how?

Personal Declaration

I am me in this moment.
I will be me in the next.
Who I was yesterday is no longer.
Who I will be tomorrow is unknown.

As one Black Woman, I am strong.
As Black Women, we are the
strongest.
Me for you and you for me,
Standing as One for all to see.

My inner being defines what you
see.
It reflects what my soul holds.
Life moves at my pace.
It flows with my thoughts.

The world around does not define
me.
That on-going task is all mine.
The Black Beauty in the mirror.
She is Me.
She is Us.

Answer to the question

All for One or All for Self?

The Black Woman is All for Self when it focuses on her finances, family, faith, and physical & mental well-being.

The Black Woman is All for One when these areas of her life allow her to connect with others and thus grow and evolve in service to them.

Henceforth, everything she is and does is for the goodness, strength, love, and well-being of other Queens.

References

Catalyst (2021). Women of Color in the United States (Quick Take). Table 1. Retrieved from https://www.catalyst.org/research/women-of-color-in-the-united-states/

Pew Research Center. (2021) Facts about the U.S. Black Population. Retrieved from https://www.pewresearch.org/social-trends/fact-sheet/facts-about-the-us-black-population/

Statista Research Department (2021). Total Population in the United States by Gender from 2010 to 2025 Table 1. Retrieved from https://www.statista.com/statistics/737923/us-population-by-gender/.

About the Author

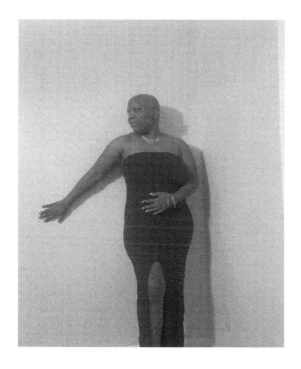

As the author of eight published books, Cathy is not new to the writing industry. Her previous books, available on Amazon and other online book retailers, are geared towards a variety of

personal development topics for females
and couples. They are listed below.
Additional books are in the works.

When she is not speaking, writing,
or spending time with her family, Cathy
is involved in volunteer activities,
enjoying a great movie, listening to
music, or watching her Dallas Cowboys.
Cathy is from North Carolina but resides
in Georgia.

Books

1. Love Your T.E.A.R.S.

2. Use Your Own Chalk

3. Footprints of an Invisible Father

4. A Queen's Manual

5. Sensual Seduction Humans

Crave

6. Why I Luv U

7. Why I Luv U 2

Contact

Website: www.mrscathywebb.com

Email: thewritewayishere@gmail.com

IG: @author_cathylwebb

FB: @author.cathylwebb

LinkedIn: @iamcathylwebb

Made in the USA
Columbia, SC
19 February 2022